Praise for Fundraising Kick

"I like that they're simple things that can be done right now to bring in some income and re-engage with donors. Simple things that I kind of know to do, but don't always make time to do...I think Fundraising Kick emails are excellent, I really do."

Michael Hodsgon
Cause4Effect, Ltd
Aberdeen, UK

"Thank you for Fundraising Kick! The one on fundraising cocktail parties was one of the most useful things I've seen as I'm trying to get members of our Trustees to host parties. It's nice to have a clear plan from an outside expert."

Robin Glossner
James V. Brown Library
Williamsport, PA

"Every week I get one of Marc's Fundraising Kick emails. They are great! The Kicks don't always pertain to my situation, but they remind me to focus on what's important."

Trisha Box
KLOVE/AIR-1 Radio
San Antonio, TX

"The Fundraising Kick emails are great. Short, sweet and useful. They definitely gave me ideas and encouragement. Thank you for making my job easier and more enjoyable."

Eli Adler
Jewish Arizonans on Campus
Phoenix, AZ

Praise for Ask Without Fear!®

"'Get REAL' will take on new meaning for board and staff members who read this book. Readable, on point, filled with memorable stories and well-tested practices, this little book is a great addition to the field of pragmatic advice to those looking for more successful engagement in fundraising."

Kay Sprinkel Grace
Principal, Transforming Philanthropy and author, Beyond Fundraising
San Francisco, CA

"I enjoyed Ask Without Fear! Marc has taken a subject that has been written about often and given it a new twist. Clearly, his effort is a work of passion and love. My hat is off to him."

Jerry Linzy, Senior Managing Partner
Panas, Linzy & Associates
Chicago, IL

"This short, practical book gives you a series of step-by-step methods to raise more money, faster and easier than you ever thought possible."

Brian Tracy, Author
The Psychology Of Selling

Praise for Ask Without Fear!® for Librarians

"Using Marc's framework, we were able to exceed our fundraising goal in the worst recession since the Great Depression."

Sarah Sugden
Library Director
Waterville Public Library

Other works by Marc A. Pitman

Ask Without Fear!

Ask Without Fear for Librarians

The Ask Without Fear! DVD set

The Ask Without Fear! DVD Board Retreat-in-a-box set

Google+ for Nonprofits

The $100,000 Guide to E-mail Solicitation

The MagnetGoals Goal Setting Workbook

Creating Donor Evangelists: Moving Donors from Mere Check Writers to Raving Fans

Who's Telling Your Story?

Fundraising Kick

A Year of Ask Kicking Ideas

Marc A. Pitman

The Fundraising Coach

Fundraising Kick : A year of ask kicking ideas
Published by The Fundraising Coach, LLC

Cover Design by Joshua Fisher
joshuafish@gmail.com

ISBN: 978-1-938079-00-9 (print)
ISBN: 978-1-938079-01-6 (ebook)

For more information, or to have Marc speak to your team or conference, contact him at:

The Fundraising Coach, LLC

8 Waterville Commons Drive, Ste 137
Waterville, ME 04901
(207) 370-2275
www.FundraisingCoach.com

Dedication

To my wife and family, thanks for giving me something worth working for.

Fundraising Kick
A year of ask kicking ideas

Table of Contents

Introduction

I've been a professional fundraiser for almost half of my life. I've seen lots of success, despite bad economies. I've even gotten to travel the world teaching other people how to ask without fear.

People pay a lot for those trainings. But I've noticed a slightly disturbing truth: ***most of the people that hire me already know how to ask for money.***

They know effective tips on writing fundraising letters. They read the right books and blogs. They go to great conferences and professional association meetings.

But they're not making the asks.

They'll be the first to tell you the #1 reason people give money is that they are asked. But they aren't making the asks!

So I created the weekly Fundraising Kick emails. It's a form of coaching, but geared to senior leaders. People who already know what to do, just need a kick to get them out making ask.

I really wanted to call the emails "Ask Kick" or "Kick Ask" but I wasn't sure if people would get their board to pay for a service like that. So I settled for the more pedestrian "Fundraising Kick."

These fundraising ideas have been used by professionals and volunteers, employees and founders. People all over the world are finding the Kicks make them raise more money.

I believe you'll find that too. This book is a compilation of the first year of Kicks. I've worked hard to keep these as true to the original emails as possible, even down to the obviously outdated travel information in my PS's. At the time of this writing, the links all are accurate. If you find them not working, please let me know by emailing me at marc@fundraisingcoach.com so I can update them.

I recommend you don't read this book all the way through. You don't need more information. You need to *act on the information you already have.*

To get the maximum benefit from these Kicks, open up to the month you are currently in, and start with one Kick. Do that activity, and then move on to the next. It would be best to set up a weekly reminder in your calendar at the start of the week to review a Kick. You'll notice most of my emails start with "Good morning!" I like sending these in the morning so people have time to schedule the action into their calendar.

These Kicks are designed to remind you what you know you need to do. Let me know what you end up doing as a result of them!

To your fundraising success!

7 December 2012
Waterville, Maine USA

PS I have loads more fundraising ideas. You can sign up for the new Kicks by going to http://FundraisingKick.com/.

JANUARY

WEEK 1: How to create an extra month of fundraising

The first Kick will come next week. But in preparation for that, think about this: **devoting just 1 hour a day to asking people for money would add up to around 250 hours a year.** *That's more than 31 work days!*

Think about that...an entire month! Can you imagine the impact devoting an entire month to fundraising would have on your nonprofit?

Even if you devoted just an hour a week, that would still be more than 6 work days!

How many asks could you make in an hour? How many major gift visits could you set up? 2? 3? 10?

So today, I challenge you to block one hour a week as a repeating event on your calendar.

And next week, we'll start in with the Kicks!!

To your fundraising success,

WEEK 2: Script for calling 10 donors

Welcome to the Fundraising Kick!

As I promised, these emails will be short and to the point. This isn't about teaching you. You already know what to do. This is about inspiring you to do it!

Did you block out one hour a week like we talked about last week?

This week, I challenge you to use that hour to call 10 people and set up face-to-face asks. All you need to do is say something like:

> "Hi, this is [your name]."
>
> [They say hi and happy New Year]
>
> "It *is* a happy New Year! In fact I'm calling to set up a time when I could tell you about a couple cool projects we're working on! I'd love to see if they are something you'd get involved with. Would your calendar permit you to get together for 20 minutes next Tuesday in the morning?"

I told you I'd do everything short of reaching through the phone and dialing for you, didn't I? *grin*

Make the words your own, but do the calls. And do them in batches of 10. They get *much* easier after 4 and 5.

In fact, why wait until your scheduled hour. I challenge you to do it now. Before you do anything else.

Let me know how it goes!

To your fundraising success,

WEEK 3: No more excuses

Here's your next Fundraising Kick!

It's the 3rd week in the year. There are no more excuses for not calling people. Holiday festivities are over and people are back from vacations.

So today, I challenge you to make a list of 10-20 people that gave a gift in calendar year before last but not last calendar year.

Now call each of them. Set up an appointment if you'd like, but it is easier to just ask them something like:

> *"As we start a new year, would you consider supporting us like you did in 2009?"*

Do it. And let me know how it goes! (Remember, it's easier to do these all in one batch of calls.

To your fundraising success,

PS If you're finding these kicks helpful, please share it with your friends: http://FundraisingKick.com/

WEEK 4: Focus on pledge payments

Welcome to Fundraising Kick!

Last week we looked at people who'd given in the previous calendar year but not last year. I bet you found some people that made pledges but missed a pledge payment. Even though most fundraising goals are counted on pledges, you know you need those pledges to come in so your nonprofit has cash flow.

Today, I challenge you to call some people who are behind on their pledge payments. Do it from an attitude of knowing they *want* to pay their pledge. You're just calling to see how you can help.

You might say something like this:

> "Hi Joe, this is [your name] calling from [your org]. I'm looking over pledges to the [X project or X fund] and noticed we hadn't received the last installment from you. Would it be easier for you if we set this up as a recurring credit card charge? Some of our donors like getting points on their card *and* making a gift to us."

or “I know the economy is still wonky, would it help if we changed your payment schedule?”

Either way, you are helping your donor with their pledge. And you are helping your organization by knowing when the receivables will come in.

Why not make 5 of these calls this week? Maybe one a day?

Be sure to let me know how it goes! I’ll bet you’ll be surprised at how grateful donors are that you called!

To your fundraising success,

WEEK 5: Don't stay comfortable!

Here's your next Fundraising Kick!

It's the 5th week of the year—only 45 left!

We've had some great experience in asking this month. But chances are you've been calling on the people that you more easily connect with.

Today, I challenge you to make a list of 8 people that are in a different category than you normally approach.

- Maybe they are people whose business success or social status intimidates you?
- Or maybe you find you connect more easily with men. This week set up visits with women.
- Or maybe you're just asking for money from people in their 60's. This week work on setting up visits with 5 people older than that range (if possible) and 5 people younger.

We need our donors to come from a diverse set of backgrounds and circumstances. Invest in diversity this week.

To your fundraising success,

PS As always, I love hearing about the successes and the struggles! Let me know how it goes!

FEBRUARY

WEEK 1: Remember to say "thank you"

Welcome to Fundraising Kick!

One month of the year is already done! Can you believe it? 11 months left!

Here in North America, Valentine's Day is one week away. So this week, I challenge you to show love to some donors:

Reach out to 8-12 people who've been regular donors and say "thank you."

You might even say:

> "Hi Sue, this is [your name].
>
> Helping my kids make Valentine's cards for their class got me thinking about the people that make [your nonprofit] special.
>
> You were one of the first to come to mind. Thank you.
>
> Thank you for your [gift/long history of support/advocacy on our behalf]. You're helping us change lives.
>
> Happy Valentine's Day!"

We all know we're supposed to say "thank you" 7 times between solicitations. So why not use this week to make some of those calls. Hand written notes are good. But make 8-12 calls too.

PS This week, leaving a voice mail is fine.

WEEK 2: Do your work and then show yourself some love

Hi all,

Once again, I couldn't get wait to get this out to you. So I'm sending it to you on Sunday night!

Since these emails are meant to get you to work on what you already know, this one will be brief.

This week, make 10 calls. 10. Calls to set up solicitation appointments. Calls to make an ask over the phone. Calls to set up tours of your organization.

But make 10 calls to people you want to see donate to your organization this year.

Then TREAT YOURSELF. Buy a latte. Get your nails done. Take a bubble bath.

After all, it's Valentine's Day this week. It's important to show yourself some love too!

Have a profitable week!

WEEK 3: Visualize success

Good morning everyone!

Welcome to a new week! As you've been making these specific asks this year, have you noticed how wonky your imagination can be?

As you reach for the phone, do you find yourself thinking you're interrupting the other person? Being a nuisance?

Well stop it.

Asking for gifts is really *giving* something to the donor. You are inviting them to be part of your cause. You really are welcoming them in.

So this week, make just 5 calls. But before each call take 30-60 seconds to mentally "see" the other person eagerly anticipating your call. See them on the edge of their seat, hoping for that ringing phone to be you calling. Make it as real as possible. How does their office look? What are they wearing?

Visualize them being incredibly grateful that you asked them for a gift. Seriously. Even if you call is just to set up an appointment, see them as being overjoyed about being asked to get involved.

Then make the call.

This may feel goofy at first. That is alright. It really is the same thing you were doing when you had the dread-filled feeling of being a nuisance. Your imagination was painting a picture.

This week, take the brush back.

You'll be amazed at the difference. Please, reply to this email and let me know how they went!

PS Yes, it is fine to make more than 5 of these calls. But make no less than 5 with the mental preparation.

WEEK 4: How can you help your donor?

Happy new week, Kickers!

This week, rather than doing a volume of calls, **let's focus on just one person and ask "How can I help her?"**

- Maybe they want to honor their parents. How can you help them? Perhaps by showing them how to set up an endowment.
- Maybe they want to make sure their kids are cared for. How can you help them? By showing them how a charitable lead trust will give your nonprofit income, give them a tax benefit, *and* leave their family with a set amount of money.
- Maybe they want to honor the life of a recently deceased pet. (Seriously.) How can you help them? Letting them know they can make a gift in memory of that pet.

These are just a few ideas. Do you see how they stay in the "Fundraising Kick" realm while shifting the focus to the donor?

The most helpful thing for your donor might be letting her personally know that her gift is truly making an impact. And thanking her.

So right now, find one person who could significantly help your nonprofit, and ask "How could I help her?"

Then do it.

To your fundraising success!

PS This isn't an automated email. I really just wrote it. And I'd love to know who you choose to help this week and how you help her!

MARCH

WEEK 1: 2 easy steps to a more effective fundraising appeal

Good morning! (I'm assuming you'll be reading this in the morning on Tuesday, not at night on Monday! *grin*)

Can you believe that TWO months of 2011 are now past?!

We've been focusing on getting out from behind your desk to ask for money because this tends to generate the largest gifts. But I don't want you to forget direct mail and other forms of asking.

This week, I challenge you to draft a fundraising appeal. One for direct mail. Here are a couple things to help you get started:

- Try to start the letter with the word "you." And try to use that word as often as you can. Using "you" will force you to write better fundraising letters.
- Use a story you've recently discovered: As a Kicker, you've done a lot of face-to-face solicitations this year. So you've heard a lot of stories. Has one particularly moved you? Use it in this appeal. (Of course, don't use identifiable details if the person hasn't given you permission!)

Even if you are fortunate enough to have someone else do your direct mail letters, surprise them with a draft of you own!

Try to get this appeal out before the middle of April. Depending on the size of your list, you might even go for a St. Patrick's Day appeal like the one I outlined on my blog: http://fundraisingcoach.com/2011/02/17/make-some-green-this-st-pattys-day/

I promised to keep these short, so I'll stop here. Please, let me know how your fundraising letter goes!

Marc

PS Thank you for the kind replies many of you have given me! If you think Fundraising Kick is helping you, please pass it on to a friend! http://FundraisingKick.com/

WEEK 2: Getting the board on board

Greetings Kickers!

I'm at a conference in Rhode Island so I'm sending this from my phone. I don't think the spell check messed up any words!

It is now the 11th week in the year. That means there are only 41 left.

Chances are good that you have some board members who haven't given any donations yet this calendar year.

This week, I challenge you to ask them all too make a gift by the end of the month.

Personally, I think you should be asking them for a minimum of $1000. A gift that shows they're prioritizing giving to your organization. (It's only about $84/month.)

If you haven't set minimum giving expectations for your board (and many haven't), you might say something like:

> "I'd like to ask you to consider giving $1000 this year. Is that even a possibility?"

If it becomes clear that it isn't, you can always say:

"No worries. We are really glad you're on the board. Your _______ [expertise with the construction, ideas about investment policy, insight into strategic planning--be specific] had been invaluable to us. We want a wide range of talents on the board so we haven't set a 'minimum'gift level. However, as you learned during orientation, we do everyone to make a gift at some level. As you know, grant makers and major givers often want to know if 100% of the board is giving financially. If we're not, they may get nervous and wonder if the board knows something that they don't."

We all ask our respective board members too give of their time, talent, and treasure. While we value all three, treasure is the easiest to report on. :)

Happy asking! Please reply to this email to let me know how it goes!

PS It goes without saying that you should make your own gift first!

WEEK 3: Can't quantify blood sweat and tears

Hi Kickers!

How did your board asks go?

This week, extend those asks to all your employees. It'll be much easier now that the board is "on board."

In asking employees, you could say something like, "Our board has all given already this year. Would you join them?"

Here's a fun idea: use candy bars to sweeten the ask. [pun fully intended]

I've had fun attaching "PayDay" candy bars to notes asking for a donation to employees who hadn't yet given. It's a fun way to remind employees of the option of giving through their paychecks. *grin*

For employees who've already given, I like sending a thank you note and including "100 Grand" bars or "Kudos" candy bars.

What's best is that people start talking with each other! Asking each other why they received different bars. *grin*

WARNING: It's VERY odd to think of making a gift to your employer. Giving BACK some of the money that is paid to you for your work. VERY odd.

I understand that. I've found it very helpful to use a "blood, sweat, & tears" reply. It goes like this:

> "I know you're already giving your blood, sweat, and tears to [your organization's name]. Thank you. I brag about the hard work of people like you every day. Unfortunately, it's really hard to quantify those bodily fluids in a way that foundations and major donors can understand. Did you know they sometimes ask how many of the employees are giving to us? Money is very easy to quantify. And a gift of any size counts. They want to hear 100% are giving, not how much the gift is for. Would you be willing to make some sort of cash gift?"

Have fun with this. As staff members learn how important their philanthropy is, they become wonderful helpers in recruiting their peers!

Marc

PS Remember to include staff in major gift recognition you do. For some reason, we often keep them out. But if they're giving at levels that qualify them as major donors, steward them too.

WEEK 4: End of the first quarter!

Hey Kickers!

It's the end of the first quarter of the calendar year!

This week, seek out someone who's already given this year and **ask their story**.

- -What caused them to give?
- -What do they like most about your cause or organization?

And be sure to ask them who else they think you should talk to?

Then go ask 3-5 new people either:

- on the list of referrals from the donor you spoke with
  OR
- -some existing prospects but using the donor's answers as the story leading to the ask

Let's finish this quarter strong!

APRIL

WEEK 1: Let's make April "Go For No" month!

Greetings Kickers!

It's fun to see this list growing. If you're finding these updates helpful, free to recommend it to others!

I'm very pleased to announce a fun competition only open to Fundraising Kick subscribers: a chance to win a free coaching session with me. Read on to find out more.

One of the most helpful books I've read in the last year is a short book called *Go for No!* http://amzn.to/gofornobook [amazon affiliate link]

The premise of the tale is that the average sales people set goals based on getting a certain number of yes's. Once they hit their goal, they stop.

But sales people that go for a certain number of no's, outperform their counterparts. When they get a yes, they keep pushing on because they need a certain number of no's.

What I like about this is that we can actually learn to like getting a no!

This week, set a goal for the number of no's you'll go for. Can you get 10? 50? 100?

The contest: If you get 100 no's this month, I'll give you a free coaching session. I don't care how you get the no's—phonathon, face-to-face asks, etc.—just as long as they're no's when you ask for money for your nonprofit.

Whether you're interested in the contest or not, definitely go for no this week. You'll be surprised at how freeing it can be!

PS I've created a card to help you. http://fundraisingcoach.com/NoCard-HalfPage.pdf

[UPDATE: Nobody won this contest the first time I issued it. But I'll extend it to readers of this book. Do it and you qualify for a free coaching session with me.]

WEEK 2: Keep going for no's

Greetings Kickers!

So, how many no's did you get? 10? 20?

===============
Details for a free recording of the "Go For No!" Seminar are below!
===============

Getting happy about no's is definitely counter-intuitive. It goes against all that we've learned.

But were you able to celebrate when you got no's last week?

Remember, anyone getting 100 no's this month gets a free coaching session with me. **This would be a great time to look over the list of people you've already asked this year.** Chances are, some of them said no. Why not pick 10 of them to follow up with this week? Think of it this way, if they say "yes"...you win. And if they say "no," you get to check another no off the sheet! *grin*

I'm honored to have talked the author of "Go For No!" into doing a free webinar:
EVENT: Go for No! for Fundraising Success
LINK: http://InstantTeleseminar.com/?eventid=18810696

Please join us!

To your fundraising success,

PS You can get the card I've created to help you track your no's at http://fundraisingcoach.com/NoCard-HalfPage.pdf

WEEK 3: Going for no changes your attitude

Hi Kickers,

I'm glad so many of you were able to be on the free "Go For No" seminar last week. If you missed it, the free replay is available at: http://instantteleseminar.com/?eventid=18810696

We've been focusing on "no's" for a couple weeks now. Are you seeing how this changes the way you go about your calls? Are you finding yourself getting, if not thrilled, at least a little pleased with a no now that no's are part of what you look for?

This week, why not **work off your "chicken list"**? Your "chicken list" is made up of people that intimidate you or that you are awe of. For some, this may be a bank president, a local celebrity, or elected official. (One client called this list her "CDIH" list since it would be a "cold day in hell" before she called them!)

It's all the people we avoid because we're afraid they'll say no.

But this month, no's are the goal! Since you're looking for no's this month, why not call 5-10 people that you've been afraid to ask? You really have nothing to lose!

Your approach doesn't need to be any different than the others calls you've made. Something as simple as:

> "Hi Frank, this is [your name] from [your charity]. I'd love to set up a time this week when I could talk to you about getting involved in the [fill in the blank] Fund. I'd LOVE to give you a tour of our place. But if that won't work, I'd be glad to come to your office. Would your schedule permit us to get together for 20 minutes Wednesday morning or Thursday afternoon?"

Let me know how these calls go!!

PS To help track your no's you can use the card at:
http://fundraisingcoach.com/NoCard-HalfPage.pdf

WEEK 4: 1/3 of the year gone

Greetings Kickers!

1/3 of the year gone. How are your goals coming along?

Our special "Go For No!" focus month is ending. There is still a week to finish up those 100 no's for the free coaching session. (You can use this card to track them: http://fundraisingcoach.com/NoCard-HalfPage.pdf)

This week, as you're reviewing your goals, spend some time looking over the last 16 weeks of solicitations and **make a list of the names of all the people you need to follow up with**: donor prospects, board members, staff, etc.

Even if you're not close to getting 100 no's, following up on these donors will help you

(1) move closer to your fundraising goal and
(2) serve as a model to other staff members in your organization

So make the list and go out and ask them!

Have a great week,

PS I realize my "kicks" got a little wordy this month. I know you're busy so I'm working hard to keep them shorter!

MAY

WEEK 1: This is a great month to do fundraising!

Greetings Kickers!

May is a terrific month to do fundraising! Here in the USA summer is in the air but graduations and weddings tend to not pick up until the end of the month and into June.

This week, as you review your donor prospect assignments, look for people that might be going away for the summer. Be sure to schedule appointments to ask them before they go!

You might say something like this:

> "Joe, before you go for the summer, I'd love to talk about the programs we'll be doing this summer and see if you'd consider investing in one of them. Could we get together for coffee this Wednesday?"

Happy fundraising!

WEEK 2: Prepare for summer visitors

Greetings Kickers!

Last week you paid particular attention to people that might be leaving for the summer. (Or the winter for those of you in the Southern Hemisphere!)

This week, start compiling a list of 5-10 people who will be *coming* to your area for the season.

Now create strategies for asking them. What do you need to do? It's probably as simple as sending a note to them saying you're looking forward to them being in the area.

Or you might want to reach out to other family members and help them get involved first.

For those of you with donor prospects far away from your immediate area, resist the temptation to ignore this kick. In your case, this week might be a great week to schedule a trip to an area where many of your donors spend the season.

This may feel like an over simplistic strategy. But fundraising is ALL about relationships. Asking is part of that but so is letting people know you're interested in them, not only their money. No one wants to feel like an ATM!

So be sure to touch each of those 5-10 people this week!

To your fundraising success,

WEEK 3: Give yourself a push for fiscal year end

Greetings Kickers,

June 30 is the end of the fiscal year for many of you. **Here's a relatively easy way to help finish the year strong.**

This week, prepare a report or have a staff member do it for you of everyone who:

(1) made a gift in the first four or five months of 2010 but
(2) haven't yet this year.

You may have to ask for a "LYBUNT" report—Last Year But Unfortunately Not This. I don't like that term but it is what it is.

Then choose 10 and ask them to give. These are pretty easy calls. Since they've already given, you're just asking them to do what they've already done. You can even save time by making these asks on the phone if you'd like.

But **these are incredibly important**—it costs a lot less money to retain a donor than to find a new donor.

If they aren't able to give as much, be sure to let them know that lower gifts would still be helpful.

Or ask them if you should come back to them again later in the year.

Happy fundraising!

WEEK 4: Gifts "in memory of" and "in honor of"

Greetings Kickers!

For many of us in the Northern Hemisphere, graduations are starting to happen. Weddings too.

As you establish your list of 5-10 asks this week, remember the power of gifts "in honor" or "in memory" of others. Perhaps grandparents will make a gift to your nonprofit "in honor" of a graduation grandchild. Or maybe someone getting married will make a gift "in memory" of a loved one who passed away before their wedding day.

The possibilities are endless. This is a great way to get your fundraising year finished well if you end on June 30. Or merely give it a mid-year bump. Anyone is fair game for this kind of ask, even people that gave last week!

And the fact that you're thinking of *them* and *their* celebrations will help remind them that you are interested in their life, not just their wallet.

Happy fundraising!

PS Next weeks will be sent on Tuesday given the holiday here in the USA.

PPS If you're getting value from Fundraising Kick, would you suggest it to a friend? You can send them to http://FundraisingCoach.com/FundraisingKick/

WEEK 5: Asking for handouts or investments?

Greetings Kickers!

We're almost half way through 2011! Time is flying!

This week, instead of asking for money, why not make a list of 5-10 people you can call and thank for their investment in your cause.

Look for something to celebrate:

- a recent article in the paper, or
- an award or recognition the organization's achieved, or
- some sort of milestone.

Then call up the people in your list and thank them. If you're really ambitious, call your board to thank them *and* call 5-10 other donors!

Not sure what to celebrate? Just get out to wherever your mission is being accomplished and harvest some stories. Hang out at the soup kitchen. Go walk a trail that your group just built. Mingle with the people your nonprofit serves.

Your call could be something like:

> "Hi Sally! This is [your name] from [your organization]. I'm calling to thank you for your support this year. Do you have a minute for me to share a story of what support like yours is helping us accomplish?"

Have fun making the calls!

JUNE

WEEK 1: Time management revisited

Good morning Kickers!

We're almost half way through the year.

Many of you have been with Fundraising Kick since we started in January. Do you remember how to add an extra month of solicitations to your year?

Devote just 1 hour a day to asking people for money!

Just one hour a day will add up to around 250 hours. (You need to take vacation and enjoy weekends!)

But 250 hours works out to more than 31 work days. Dedicated solely in fundraising! *Can you imagine what that would do for you fundraising program?*

This week, I challenge you to revisit your schedule. Do you think you can add an hour a day for fundraising? Or even block one hour a week? In a year, one hour a week would add up to more than 6 working days of 100% solid fundraising.

Remember, Fundraising Kick is designed to give you the kick to do what you already know how to do. Blocking out time on your calendar will give you the space to take that action!

To your fundraising success!

WEEK 2: Reconnect with the locals

Good afternoon, Kickers!

If you live in an area that sees seasonal residents, take this week to reconnect with the 5-10 "locals." Ask them for a gift to your cause. But also ask them who of the seasonal residents they suggest you talk to and why.

That way, you'll have another 5-10 asks to work on in the coming weeks. With seasonal folks, you have to have a strategic plan. Asking locals now will give you the necessary lead time. (If your seasonal visitors come in 6 months, this will give you a LOT of lead time.)

To set up these visits, you could say something like:

> "Sally, would you have 20-30 minutes on Thursday? I'd love to talk to you about our cause and who of the Snow Birds [or whatever you call them] we should be approaching."

Happy asking!

Marc

WEEK 3: How to hold a fundraising houseparty

Good morning Kickers!

Here's a quick idea for you: cocktail parties. Cocktail parties can be VERY effective way to ask for money or just spread the word about your cause!

This week, I challenge you to approach 5 board members and ask them to each host a reception at their house. These can be done in 90 minutes and don't need to cost the hosts too much in the way of food or drink. And they're great at just about any time of the year!

To help you, I've included a detailed plan of a cocktail party below. It's long, but I think you'll find it as helpful as my other coaching clients have.

To your fundraising success!

How to Hold a Fundraising House Party

Regular cocktail parties in other people's homes should be an important part of your calendar. This is a low-level, one-time way for people to take significant action on behalf of your nonprofit. It's particularly good for board members to do these, as well as other influential people in your community.

Here's what such an event might look like:

6:00-6:30 pm People arrive, mingle, & nosh (maybe wine/beer and cheese & crackers or heavier hors d'oeuvres)

6:30 Welcome from host, share why your nonprofit is so important to them personally, introduce executive director or board chair

6:40 Executive director or board chair make a few comments or introduces video (if you have one)

6:50 Executive director or board chair follows up video with 3 specific gift amounts that make sense to your cause. If you were a spay/neuter clinic, you might say "As you can see, we are partnering with the humane societies and the rescue shelters. We're the ounce of prevention for their pound of cure. But we need your help:

- $10,000 will fund a month of surgeries to low-income families needing financial assistance
- $5000 would sponsor a day of surgeries, preventing hundreds of animals from needing to be euthanized each day
- $1000 will sponsor a surgery a month for the year

OR

An alternative way could be to bill this as "no fundraising at the event." In that case, you'd leave them with some materials and let them know that the host or a member of the staff would be following up with them in the next week or so.

OR

A third way to do this is to not ask for money at all. Simply use these to introduce people to your cause. You might ask them to volunteer or become advocates and give them ways to do both.

7:00 Host wraps up, if not a solicitation event s/he can thank everyone for coming, and encourage them to take information as they leave "This is a great organization. Thank you all for coming. Executive director/board chair will be here to answer questions. Please help us finish up the food."

OR (better)

The host says, "We believe in this so much, we're giving $x,xxx to do _____. We ask that each of you would consider doing that too."

OR

A plant in the crowd says, "I want to sponsor a day. I have my check book right here and will commit to doing that."

7:10 More mingling and chatter as folks ask questions and start leaving.

I wouldn't do a Q&A after the video unless you get a real sense that the group will give a lively discussion. The awkward pause of waiting for the first question is often a momentum killer at an event.

These could be used as purely informational sessions too. But I advise you do them as solicitation events.

WEEK 4: MAKE CALLS!

Greetings Kickers!

This is it: you're half way through the calendar year.

This week: MAKE CALLS.

People respond well to deadlines. June 30 is a great deadline, either as half way through the calendar year or as the end of your fiscal year.

This is the week to give your fundraising a final push.

Whether you fiscal year ends this month or not, **dedicate this week to making 20-30 fundraising calls.** Call:

1. People that haven't yet given
2. People that haven't given in a few years
3. People that might give to a special project you're doing
4. People that gave in the fall (they just might give again this month)
5. Board and employees that haven't given

Honestly, you could even make "cold" calls to people that have no history of supporting you.

Be prepared, making the 20-30 calls will take a lot of time. Schedule that in your calendar right now.

Making voice contact with this many people will be VERY good for your development effort. Even if you don't get the cash in the next 3 days, you will set yourself up for having more fundraising success in July!

To your fundraising success,

PS Next FRKick will be on Tuesday or Wednesday. July 4 is a holiday here in the USA.

JULY

WEEK 1: Corporate donors and foundations

Happy New (Fiscal) Year, Kickers!

Many of you started a new fiscal year on Friday. (If you haven't seen it yet, I did a video "thank you" for fundraisers like you: http://bit.ly/luoeu7)

Whether or not you started a new fiscal year, take some of you "asking" time this week to reflect and plan.

In particular, look over the mix of donors you've had in the last 12 months. Overall, **it's typical for 80% of the donors to be people, not corporations or foundations.** And here on Fundraising Kick, we tend to focus on getting out and reaching those individuals.

This week, take a look at the corporations and foundations that are making gifts. Make a list of 5-10 to contact. Since these donors usually have gatekeepers, why not handwrite thank you notes to each of them?

The great news is: foundations and corporations are run by...*people*. Saying "thanks" can make you stand out. Not a scheduled follow up. Just an "out of the blue" thank you.

If you're really ambitious, choose 5-10 others that gave in fiscal year before the most recent fiscal year but aren't on your first list. And thank them.

Happy thanking!

PS I see Fundraising Kick as a conversation. Please let me know how you put these tips into practice!

WEEK 2: Draft your upcoming fundraising appeals

Hi again, Kickers!

Summer (for those of us in the Northern Hemisphere) is a great time to do some advance planning.

This week, I challenge you to draft out your next 2-3 direct mail appeals. Calendar year end (Dec 31st) may feel like a long way away, but it'll be here before you know it. And you need to build in lead-time for direct mail houses or volunteers to process the mailing of your letters.

So this week:

- **Choose the dates for your letters.**
  I recommend getting them out
  - in late August/early September (say 8/28)
  - November, just before Thanksgiving (maybe 11/15)
  - and mid-to-late December (maybe 12/23 or 12/26)

  Three is ambitious. You might only get 2 or even 1. I'd strongly recommend you get at least 2 out, beginning of the school year and end of the calendar year.

- **Figure out how much time they need for processing**
  Ask your staff member or, since most of you are in small shops, call the mail house to see when they need the files in order to be able to drop them in the mail on the date you want. Put those dates on the calendar.

- **Then start writing the letters! THIS WEEK!**

There is no rule saying you have to write the letters close to their drop date. *So draft all three now*. Make it as complete as possible. You might find this blog post on how to write fundraising letters helpful: http://fundraisingcoach.com/2011/02/01/how-to-write-effective-fundraising-letters/

Trust me, getting it done now will make the next the last months of this year MUCH less stressful!

To your fundraising success,

WEEK 3: Harvest from your lists

Greetings Kickers!

If you're like many of us, you get bursts of ideas, make lots of lists, feel good about it, and then move on with your life, never looking at your lists again.

This week, give yourself an hour to go over all those lists. You might call it "harvesting."

Review these lists with an eye to who you can contact for support. Maybe there are people you've asked but haven't heard back from? Or great prospects that you simply haven't approached yet?

Harvest these names and pull them into *another* list and *ask them this week*. At least 5, preferably 10.

Happy fundraising!

Marc

PS If you've been on FR Kick for a while, be sure to include the lists you've made in response to these emails too!

WEEK 4: Visiting donors in their "natural habitat"

Hello Kickers!

These short, swift emails are designed to get you asking for support for your cause.

Much of that can be done from behind your desk. But this week, go away. ☺

Go out to where your donors are. Visit them in their "natural habitat." This week:

- visit their stores
- go to the café or restaurants they go to
- walk your downtown, paying attention for regular donors

You could even ask a donor for a tour of their factory. Some of my best visits have been just this. Tours remind donors (and you) that they are human beings, not ATM banking machines.

You could say something like:

> "Hi Nancy, this is [your name]. I know you run XYZ Manufacturing, but I realized I don't have any idea how that gets done! Would I be able to have a tour of your facility?"

TWO POINTS

1. Many of you work for charities with a larger donor base. So you might not see your board or donors if you walk around downtown. Do it anyway. Try to choose the "natural habitat" for your typical donors.

2. As you see donors, tour their facility, or explore habitats similar to theirs, be open to names of people that you should solicit this week. Be sure to have a small notebook (I like the little Moleskine ones.) Jot down names that come to mind.

When you have 5-10 names, whip out your cell phone or run back to your office to call them!

Remember: No money, no mission. No asking, no money.

Get out there and ask! ☺

PS Remember, I'm as close as a "reply" to this email. Please let me know how this goes!

AUGUST

WEEK 1: Sharpen the saw

Morning Kickers!

Welcome to August!

We worked hard last month! Together we:

- harvested names from all the lists we've made since January (I uncovered 45 people to call back!)
- drafted the appeals for the next 12 months and started writing the fall & year end appeals
- identified corporations and foundations to solicit
- and walked around in donors' "natural habitat"

In *7 Habits of Highly Effective People*, Stephen Covey talks about the importance of "Habit 7: Sharpening the Saw."

He tells a story of two woodsmen in a tree sawing contest. The first woodsman sawed trees non-stop. As soon as one tree was felled, he moved on to the next. He took an early lead and, as the day went on, laughed at his opponent.

For his opponent was stopping at regular intervals to sharpen and oil his saw. But at as the day came to a close, the first man was having to work harder, strain his muscles more, to get his saw to work on trees. His opponent? His saw, being as sharp as the beginning of the day, was felling more trees with less strain.

The point is obvious, if we keep working at screech, we'll actually be *less* effective than if we take some time to regroup, to "sharpen the saw." Covey talks about sharpening the saw weekly by setting goals in four areas: physical, social/emotional, mental, and spiritual. You can read about that here: https://www.stephencovey.com/7habits/7habits-habit7.php

The end of the year will be here before we know it. Can you take some time this week to sharpen the saw? I'm talking about taking a day or two off. If you can't this week, take time this week to schedule some "saw sharpening" time on your calendar. Here are some ideas:

- One friend aims to take the first Monday of each month as a study day.
- Another tries to be sure to take long weekends this month to spend with family and friends.
- Yet another, treats herself to vanilla lattes after a successful solicitation.

What about you? What can you do? Read the information at the link above. What can you do each week to make sure that you're habitually sharpening the saw?

One of the worst things for fundraisers is to be all work and no play. People can't relate to that. And to be an effective fundraiser, you need to be able to relate to people.

Let me know, how do *you* sharpen the saw? Reply to this email to let me know!

PS If this isn't a week to take vacation time, be sure to schedule time ask 5-10 people! You could get a jump start on next week by asking people that might be leaving your area at the end of the summer (or winter if you're in the other hemisphere!).

WEEK 2: Prospects on the move

Morning Kickers!

Were you able to identify some ways to sharpen the saw?

This week, take advantage of the changing of the season. Summer is ending here in the northern hemisphere. List 5-10 donors or prospects that are either

- going to leave your area (if people summer where you are) OR
- will be coming back

Map out some ways to set up appointments or to move them a step closer to an ask.

Then call all 5-10!

PS I'll be in Bowling Green, KY doing a training for WKU and then in Chattanooga, TN speaking at the Tennessee Valley Institute for Nonprofit Excellence. Let me know if you're in either area. I'd love to connect!

WEEK 3: Creating a matching fund

Morning Kickers!

August is flying by too, isn't it?

This week, look over past years' giving reports to see who you expect to make major gifts between now and December 31.

Contact 5-10 of the largest donors to set up an appointment. At the appointment, thank the person for their gift last year (or in previous years) and **ask if they'd give early this year so their gift could be used as a matching incentive for others**.

You might say something like:

> "Joe, we are so grateful for your tendency of giving $5,000 towards the end of each year.
>
> [Even if they've only done that a couple times in 5 years, that can be a "tendency." Many donors don't realize how much time goes between gifts.]
>
> I'm not sure if you plan on doing that again this year...but if you are, would you consider giving it now, or making the pledge now, so we can use it as a 'matching' incentive? Our donors tend to

be more generous when their gifts are matched dollar-for-dollar. Your early gift or pledge would help us do that."

If you don't have a matching gift policy or experience, this might feel scary. But people really do respond well to matching challenges.

This will help position you to raise even more this year end!

Marc

WEEK 4: Don't grow weary

Morning Kickers,

I hope your August is going well. Don't be discouraged if your fundraising attempts aren't yielding the gifts you'd like. It is summer. People are not in their normal work rhythm. **But all of your work is laying the groundwork for those gifts to come in before year end.**

Honestly. You are positioning yourself VERY well!

This week, look at 5-10 more people that typically give sizeable gifts at year-end and ask if they'll join the people you asked last week, adding to the matching funds. Be sure to include board members and staff as well.

To your fundraising success,

PS For those of you in the Northern Hemisphere, can you detect the shift to "normalcy" in the lives of people around you? The start of school still wields a heavy influence on many of our rhythms!

WEEK 5: The year is almost 2/3 over!

Morning Kickers,

The year is almost 2/3 over! Can you believe it?

Don't worry if your fundraising isn't 2/3 of the way over just yet. Many organizations see a disproportionate boost in fundraising at the end of the calendar year, some even seeing 50% of giving on the last day of December!

So don't grow weary in asking. You are creating funding for your organization, allowing your charity to impact people in ways no individual could do on their own.

This week, as you solicit 5-10 more people, remember to ask them for referrals. You might say something like:

> "Sally, I'm so glad we met toady. Thank you for your investment in our cause. [Or "thank you for your kind words" – if they didn't give yet.] Who else on your [fill in the blank] should we be approaching?"

Don't just ask, "who else should we ask?"—their minds will go blank. So help them:

- who else on your bowling team
- who else at your country club
- who else in your neighborhood

- who else at your church

For some reason, making the group more restricted frees the brain up to think of names. Oddly, if the person gives names, they'll often *not* be in the group you suggested. It's as though the limits give the brain freedom to think creatively.

Get out there and ask!

PS Remember, a "no" is often really a "not now." Check out this Movie Mondays video that illustrates this point perfectly: http://bit.ly/r2ATDU

SEPTEMBER

WEEK 1: A bonus kick

Hi Kickers,

Here's a bonus Kick.

Next Monday is a holiday here in the USA. But fundraising folks are generally bad about taking vacations. And when we do, we're usually carrying the weight of our goals around with us, ruining the potential rest we might have gotten by a day off.

But we do need to take breaks, to rest, to recharge.

So today, right now, list out the 3 things that, if you accomplish today, will make you feel comfortable taking Monday off.

Right now.

They could be the most urgent. Or the most important. (Not always the same thing!)

They could be things you can finish today. Or things you can move forward and pass off to someone else.

But list 3 and get them done.

Enjoy Monday!

PS Due to the holiday here in the USA, next week's Kick will come later in the week. I'll be taking a day off. *grin*

WEEK 2: Capitalize on normalcy

Hi Kickers!

Welcome to September—were you able to take Monday off? If not, be sure to schedule time off before the end of October! November and December get *very* busy!

September is a great month to fundraise! Here in the Northern Hemisphere, people are "getting back to business" with the regular rhythms of work and school. Isn't interesting that this "normalcy" even affects people without children?

So capitalize on it. If you haven't gotten a fall fundraising appeal out yet, get the copy done this week so it can be processed and mailed before the end of September.

For the rest of the month, I'll give you quick, short, practical tips on how to make the next four months the best fundraising season for your nonprofit!

To your fundraising success!

PS Check out this short video on how to work with your board. There are great tips including one toward the end about how to comfortably involve board members in asking. You can see the free video at
http://bit.ly/501Alford

WEEK 3: Are you being sexist?

Good morning Kickers!

When you signed up, I *promised* to make these short. Sort of a swift kick!

As you're looking at making the rest of the fall the best for your nonprofit's fundraising, look at your recent face-to-face visits. (In my experience, face-to-face visits is where the big money is.)

As you look at the appointments, ask yourself, "Am I being sexist?"

Are you? Are you tending to meet with men more than women? Or more women than men?

If you *are* being sexist, it's better to be having more visits with women than men. Women tend to make money decisions in families. And women tend to live longer than men, so you have more time to build a relationship.

But this week, right now, as you list out the 5-10 people you'll be calling to set up visits with, try to make sure to balance it by gender.

To your fundraising success!

PS Of course, if the decisions involve a couple, the best thing is to meet with both of them at the same time whenever that's possible!

WEEK 4: Ask for money AND volunteers

Good morning, Kickers!

Last week I saw an interesting video about a development director who saw his major task *not* as raising money, but as recruiting volunteers. His experience shows increased fundraising!

You can see the free video here: http://bit.ly/nCTWOU

I'm not sure your board or boss will totally agree. But recruiting others to expand your efforts IS important.

So as you pull together your list of 5-10 asks this week, have an eye to not only asking for money, but for recruiting volunteers to help ask also.

To your fundraising success!

P.S. There's also an interesting video from the Alford group on why big boards are better. Do you agree? http://bit.ly/uYFtdF

WEEK 5: Is your donors' house on fire?

Good morning Kickers!

Last week, Seth Godin wrote a brief post called "Can't watch your parade if the house is on fire." You can read it at: http://sethgodin.typepad.com/seths_blog/2011/09/cant-watch-your-parade-if-the-house-is-on-fire.html

It's basically a reminder that no one cares how much you know until they know how much you care.

If your donors are feeling pain with this current economy, it will be harder for them to "see your parade."

So as you cull your list for 5-10 appointments to set up, be thinking about what pain they may be in.

WARNING: DON'T LET THIS STOP YOU FROM CALLING.

As hard as it is to believe, not everyone is experiencing a bad economy. So don't be too quick to color the water. But as you meet with people, give them the chance to share their story first. Once you've heard it, they'll be in a much better place to hear yours.

Keep asking!

Marc

PS Seth's post has the song by Smash Mouth called "All star" running through my head: "my world's on fire, how 'bout yours? That's the way I like it 'cause I never get bored."

PPS Welcome to the new Kickers! As a reminder, these are intentionally short emails written for people who already know how to fundraise, they just need a kick to get them out there doing it. Please feel free to share with me how they're helping. All you need to do is reply to this email.

OCTOBER

WEEK 1: Write those November and December appeals TODAY

Good afternoon Kickers!

If you haven't worked on your mid-November and year-end appeals, *do it now.*

Seriously. **In countries around the world, we're moving into the *most generous* time of the year.**

Make sure you have mail and return envelopes in the homes of your supporters so they can send you back money!

I don't normally say this...but if you have to make the choice between writing the two letters or having one-on-one solicitations with your 5-10 people, **write the letters.**

This blog post has some tips on helping you craft your letters:
http://fundraisingcoach.com/2011/09/13/3-tips-for-effective-fundraising-letters/

To your fundraising success!

WEEK 2: Give social proof

Do donors have "proof" that you're a good investment?

Hi Kickers!

Do you donors have "proof" that you're a good investment? What sort of proof do you offer?

- statistics of growth?
- costs of overhead vs overall expenses?
- stories of changed lives?

Those are fine, but studies are showing that some of the most important proof for people making a decision is *social proof.*

Social proof is basically seeing that other people like them are doing exactly what they are considering doing.

Social proof helps reduce the risk of taking the action they're about to take. It makes giving a donation much easier.

I wrote about an example of Red Box generating social proof—they're asking people to take pictures of themselves *hugging Red Boxes!* They'll have thousands of pictures of people just like you and me hugging the boxes. You can read it here:

http://fundraisingcoach.com/2011/09/18/are-you-as-creative-as-red-box/

That same week, the folks over at Cause Effect did a blog post on social proof: http://archive.aweber.com/ceffect/BzvSI/h/Surprising_science_of_persuasion.htm

So what can you do to make sure others have social proof of supporting you? Donor lists are a start. But here are 3 powerful ways to show social proof:

1. **Use pictures of other donors**
   Make sure your publications, website, and other communications have pictures of other donors in them.

2. **Use social media to get "likes" for your organization's page**
   Did you know that sites like Facebook optimize their pages so that visitors see faces of people they know? So if you optimize likes, people checking you out will be likely to see their friends who like you too. Social proof!

3. Perhaps the ultimate form of social proof would be to **take a volunteer with you on a call**! Someone the person knows sitting with you in a room can be incredibly powerful social proof.

As you set up your 5-10 visits this week, consider asking a board member to come along with you!

I'd love to hear how you use social proof. Just reply to this email to let me know.

To your fundraising success,

Marc

WEEK 3: Get at least one house meeting before Thanksgiving

Good morning, Kickers!

This week, create your list of 5-10 asks to make. Then review that list to see who could host a house party in the next four weeks. Set up your appointment. Make your ask. And when they've indicated a gift or promised commitment, say something like:

> *"Thank you so much, Frank. You know, we're looking to do at least one more home gathering before Thanksgiving [or mid-November if that wording works better]. Would you consider hosting one?"*
>
> *Frank: "I don't know, what's that involve?"*
>
> *You: "Hosts simply open up their home and invite people they know to come meet our Executive Director. There can be a fundraising component. But it's helpful to simply meet new people too. A house party takes about an hour."*

That's about it. We're moving into the very best fundraising time of the year. Getting in front of new people now can reap huge rewards for your nonprofit!

To your fundraising success!

PS A few weeks back I sent out an outline of a house party. If you'd like it again, simply reply to this email and ask. I'll get it to you.

WEEK 4: Stick to the basics

Good Evening Kickers!

I'm thrilled with the new Kickers joining our ranks!

This month, we've looked at

- drafting 2 letters for mailing in November & December
- providing social proof for your donors that your organization is a good investment
- and getting one or two house parties before mid-November.

This week, clean up those assignments. And get back to basics. 5-10 major gift asks.

You already know what to do. Be sure to do it! Many people are feeling very open to being generous right now. Go out and find them!

To your fundraising success,

PS I'm not making this up. I'm working on a campaign in New Hampshire. Last week we closed on a $25,000 gift, a $10,000 gift, and a

$500,000 gift. Granted, these are pledges over 5 years. But each is in addition to their annual fund gift. And each year is much more than they'd previously done.

PPS Next week I'm speaking at the World Fundraising Summit in Monterrey, Mexico and then at Blog World Expo in Los Angeles. If you're near either city, let me know. I'd love to connect with you!

NOVEMBER

WEEK 1: A challenging Kick this week: don't limit your pool

Good morning, Kickers!

This morning I'm writing to you from Monterrey, Mexico. Much sunnier than my home in Maine!

This week, I have a three step challenge Kick for you.

> **(1) Quickly write out the list of 5-10 major gift prospects** you can ask for money this week.
>
> **(2) Now review that list**. What are the commonalities with these people? What makes them comfortable to call on?
>
> **(3) Now take the time to write out a list of 5-10 people who are the *polar opposites*.** As you do this, figure out where the common values are. Even if you don't like these people, where can you connect with these people? Where is the common ground?

You see, we often gravitate to the people we like, we find comfortable. The people who are enjoyable to visit. This is fine...as long as we also ask the people we don't enjoy so much.

Our charities need funding—from both those we like and those that we like less.

This week, do the hard work of reaching out to those you find a bit draining.

Your cause is worth it!

WEEK 2: Make sure your online house is in order

Good Evening Kickers!

Here in our Fundraising Kicks, we often talk about face to face asking and some direct mail asking.

This week, make sure your online house is in order.

These last two months are the busiest for most of us. And increasingly, the gifts are coming online.

Testing you system is easy: make a gift.

Really.

1. **Go to your site, trying to forget that you know about your nonprofit**
   Can you easily find wear to donate? (Check it both from the home page and from some other random page.)

2. **Make the gift**
   Can you get to the place to enter your credit card information within only 1 to 2 clicks from any page?
   How long does it take to enter your information?

Is there any way you can make the form shorter?

3. **How does it feel?**
   Does the gift go through quickly? Do you get thanked on the site? And in an email? How long does take to for you to get an acknowledgement in the mail?

Then try making small gifts on 5-10 other nonprofit sites. What can you use from those sites to make yours better?

Happy clicking,

Marc

PS Fundraising Coach is on Google+! Check it out at: https://plus.google.com/b/111031962819343975337/ It's a start! ☺

WEEK 3: An easy fundraising idea from Zappos

Hi there, Kickers!

Two weeks ago, I got an email that got me thinking "why couldn't nonprofits do that?"

Here is the entire text of the email:

> *Dear Marc Pitman,*
>
> *One year ago, you ordered the following product from Zappos.com:*
>
> *Levi's® Mens 560™ Comfort Fit - Light Stonewash - 38/29*
>
> *We wanted to let you know that right now, your size is still available*
> *from Zappos.com. You can order the same product again by visiting:*

And then came links to the exact product and another to the entire Levi's line.

How simple is that?!

Why can't you experiment with that this week?

- Run a report of everyone that gave last November
- Send those people a "one year ago" email

"One year ago, you gave a donation of ______. Thank you! We've been able to do remarkable things because of it: [list a few things as bullets]. If you'd like to help us do that over the next 12 months, would you donate again? You can do that conveniently online at: ____"

- Link to donation page

Let me know how it goes!

To you fundraising success,

PS I'd love to come work with your team in 2012. Reply to this email to see if we can work something out!

WEEK 4: Giving thanks includes thanking yourself

Morning Kickers!

This is one of my *favorite* weeks of the year. Here in the USA, we're about to celebrate Thanksgiving.

Something about this week relaxes me. Maybe it's the day off. Maybe it's the focus on thanks, gratititude, and gratefulness. Maybe it's the promise of coming New Year, a sort of "fresh start."

Whatever it is, it got me thinking about those of us who are Kickers. We already know how to raise money. And we often think about it, even off the job. Evenings. Weekends.

This week, wherever you are, allow yourself to take a break. Rest in the knowledge that you really are doing the best you can do. And rest in the reality that there are thousands of generous people out there looking for a cause like yours.

This isn't irresponsibility. This is personal leadership. All focus on money and no break makes you a very boring fundraiser. So stop. Even if only for a day, give yourself thanks for your hard work.

You're the only person that can give yourself the permission to truly take a break.

Happy Thanksgiving!

PS I'd love to hear how you take a break. For my family and I, it involves visiting one of our favorite families down on Long Island. What do you do?

WEEK 5: Double donations in December by doing this simple plan this week

Greetings Kickers!

There are 5 weeks left in the calendar year. **For donors around the world, this is when they are most generous. *And* the most distracted.** Holiday parties, year end events, business goals, family all compete for their attention.

This week, can you cash in on any of those donors we talked about in October? The ones that would set up a challenge match for year-end gifts? A dollar-for-dollar match works extremely well in motivating others to give.

If not, either try to come up with a list of 5-10 people you can call this week.

You really don't need a well thought out plan. You can call and say something like:

> "Hi Hermione, this is [your name]. I've got a sort of [crazy, out-of-the-box, different] idea that I'd love to run past you. December is a big fundraising month for [your nonprofit]. And I'm looking for 5 leaders who'd make it even bigger. These 5 leaders would contribute [$1000, $2500, $!0,000] extra to create a matching fund.

> Would you be interested in being one of the 5?"

I'd recommend the fund doubles all gifts that come in in December. If this takes off, you can send out one last appeal with the awesome news that gifts will be doubled. If it doesn't, you've still made contact with your top prospects and let them know that you consider them to be both leaders in your community *and* "insiders" for your nonprofit.

Either way, you win.

To YOUR fundraising success!

DECEMBER

WEEK 1: A simple way to get your Facebook update seen by more people

Good morning Kickers!

How did the matching gift thing idea go last week? Did you have any takers? One of my clients found this to be a fun way to put fresh energy into asks that seemed to have gone stale.

This week, I thought we'd do just a simply social media exercise. Social media isn't bringing in the money that direct asking and direct mail is, *but* most donors research their gifts before giving. And social media like Google+, Facebook, and Twitter make themselves extremely "findable" for search engines.

I'm a huge fan of Google+ and Twitter, but let's look at Facebook today.

HOW TO HELP MAKE YOUR PAGE UPDATES REACH AS MANY PEOPLE AS POSSIBLE

Facebook keeps tweaking the algorithm that determines what gets into peoples newsfeed. But one of the constants seems to be: the more people interact with an update (like, comment, and share it) the more people Facebook pushes it out to.

This becomes a virtuous cycle. You post. Facebook puts it into newsfeeds. People comment, like, and share it. So Facebook pushes it into even more people's newsfeeds allowing MORE people to like, comment, and share it.

GETTING MORE LIKES

As much as I wish people would interact with our organizational updates and the blog links we share, they don't.

People on social media tend to respond well humor and quirkiness. And quotations.

This week, get together with your team and come up with quirky questions you can ask your followers. One chocolate dessert fundraising event just posted "Mousse or cake" to their Facebook page and got a firestorm of fun comments! Another animal clinic posts fun "this or that" posts about dogs. You'd be surprised about how verbal people get about dogs.

The questions don't even have to be mission related. One organization asked if their fans were more interested in the World Series or the Super Bowl. Not only did they get a lot of replies, they also found out most of their fans were football people—that type of demographic research can be really helpful!

What are 10 questions you can ask your base?

QUOTATIONS

And remember quotations. One of the things I

get the most shares and likes and retweets on are the quotes from my book Ask Without Fear! You can see them all at: http://fundraisingcoach.com/quotes/ (In Twitter, I use a hashtag #awfquotes to help "label" them for people that don't know the book.)

These quotations can be mission related or "merely" inspirational and leadership related. If you're also posting these on Twitter and LinkedIn, try to make them no longer than 120 characters. That way people can retweet them to their followers too. (Retweets help you get exposure outside of your own fan base.)

Those two tasks are fun to work on, and they can be incredibly important in helping you reach more people in 2012!

To your fundraising success,

Marc

PS If you want to connect on these platforms, here are my links:
Facebook profile:
http://facebook.com/marcapitman
Facebook page:
http://facebook.com/askwithoutfear
Twitter: http://twitter.com/marcapitman
LinkedIn: http://linkedin.com/in/marcapitman

Google+ profile:
https://plus.google.com/u/0/11002021079320
0048119/
Google+ pages:
https://plus.google.com/u/0/b/111031962819
343975337/111031962819343975337/
and
https://plus.google.com/u/0/b/117504115740
256437836/117504115740256437836/

WEEK 2: Why this week is the BEST week to make donor appointments

Morning Kickers!

I've just heard my first "Let's get together after the 1st." Have you started hearing that?

Those of you who've been Kickers for a while know that I am a proponent of vacations, rest, and fun. But don't do that this week. The temptations are all around you. But save them until next week.

This week, do what other people won't do. Set up more appointments to solicit.

Take advantage of the fact that many people have begun to coast-to-the-new-year. Since they've started coasting, they may feel they have more time for you. (I already have tomorrow PACKED with appointments for a capital campaign I'm working on!)

So this week:

(1) Make a list of 5-10 people you wish had given this year.
(2) Set up appointments with them for this week or next. You might say something like: "Sue, this is [your name] from [your organization]. Could we get together for 20

minutes this week or next? I'd like to share with you some exciting progress we've made."

(3) If you don't have a list of "exciting projects" make a few quick calls. Check with your CFO (really!), senior leaders (if you have any), and some board members. You could ask them: "With all that's happened here since January, what sticks out the most? What seems the coolest?"

(4) At your appointments share a couple of these examples and ask them to consider making a gift of [$100? $1000? $10,000? whatever fits your organization] before December 31.

Many people won't be willing to do that this week. And that is EXACTLY why this week may be the BEST week to make appointments this year!

If you do what other people won't do, you can have what other people won't have!

To your fundraising success!

WEEK 3: A PS can help you raise money in these last 2 weeks of the year

Hi Kickers!

The end of the year is coming! At this point, try tying up loose ends.

Go for one last contact with people that haven't given. A note would be great. With a return envelope.

You could use a post script might read:

> *P.S. I've included an envelope on the off chance you'll be able to make a gift before December 31st. ☺*

It's even better if you can reference a giving level.

> "...make a President's Club gift before December 31st..."

That gives the dollar amount you were looking for.

Remember: 30% of giving happens in December.

And much of that happens in these next two weeks. Giving top prospects an envelope can be a great service to them at this busy time of the year!

To your fundraising success,

PS As we approach 2012, I'd love to know: what do you do to get ready for the new year? Do you have any personal rituals that you do? Or any systems for your professional goals? Just reply to this email (it only goes to me!).

WEEK 4: 5 specific tips to make a final push this week

Festive Greetings Kickers!

No matter what you celebrate, I hope you get to take a little time off this week. *But Kickers like you won't take the whole week off!*

December is the biggest giving month of the year. Some studies show 30% of all giving happens this year.

And THIS WEEK is a huge giving week. Christmas is over but there are still a few days before the end of the tax year. People are motivated by deadlines. And the end of the calendar year is a HUGE deadline.

Use it to you advantage.

(1) Remember to **change your voice mail** like I mentioned last week. Be sure to:

- give donors a way to contact you
- tell them when you'll be in the office and
- to point them to both the donation form and the stock transfer information form on you site. (You do have stock transfer information on your site right?)

(2) **Write a few notes to people on your "chicken list"**—the list of people you'd love to contact but are just too chicken. Send them something like "in this season of thankfulness, I just wanted to say thanks for your [support of our community, work in our cause area, show of support to the (name of another nonprofit)]. Your efforts are noticed and appreciated. Thank you!"

(3) Spend a couple days in the office. They don't have to be full days, but be sure to be in a couple of days. Chances are no one will just "show up." But if you DON'T spend time in the office, you KNOW someone will try. ☺

(4) If you use social media, be sure to schedule one or two "there's still time to make a year end gift to us" messages.
- 1 a day for Facebook and Google+ is fine. You can get away with 2 a day on Twitter.
- Experiment with posting during work hours and after hours to see what gets the most traction.
- Be sure to email some of your more active social media folks and ask if they'd like, +1, or retweet your posts.

(That will help your posts get seen by even more people.)

- Try to come up with a better call to action than “there’s still time.” (See comments in the next point on email.)

(5) Do send at least one blast to your email list. It’s up to you if you send it only to people who haven’t given yet this year or if you send it to everyone. *But avoid subjects like “Still more time to give.”* Their inboxes will be filled with them. Try to lead with a reminder of the importance of your mission. “Feed 6 more kids before Dec 31!” would be good.

Lots of money will be given away this week. Some simply because people are feeling generous. Some because people are thinking strategically about their tax situation. So just like you would for a leaky roof, make sure you put out as many buckets as you can to catch it all!

To the end of a successful fundraising year!

More Resources

From the Kindle Store

Ask Without Fear! Connecting donors with what matters to them most
http://amzn.to/rCv0Rq

Who's Telling Your (Nonprofit's) Story?
http://amzn.to/viblI2

In your email

Fundraising Kick weekly emails
http://FundraisingKick.com/

Free fundraising ideas list
http://fundraisingcoach.com/subscribe/

On the web

Movie Mondays: free nonprofit fundraising and marketing videos every week
http://MovieMondays2.com/

Free training videos:
http://www.youtube.com/user/sbsmarc

Charity How-To Webinars
http://CharityWebinars.com/

About the Author

Internationally acclaimed speaker and fundraising coach Marc A. Pitman is the founder of www.FundraisingCoach.com. He loves asking people for money and is often heard saying, "Fundraising is an extreme sport!"

A recognized thought leader, Marc has appeared in publications around the world. His leadership coaching and fundraising expertise has been seen on TV stations as diverse as Fox News and Al Jazeera and heard on radio programs around the world. His energetic and engaging keynotes and trainings have brought him to conferences and nonprofits all over the world, including New Zealand, Mexico, and Bermuda.

His FundraisingCoach.com blog is read by thousands of people around the world each month and is recognized as one of the top 10 nonprofit training blogs in the world. His clients call him an "approachable expert" that helps them reconnect with the passion that got them into fundraising in the first place.

That passion has inspired people to translate his book *Ask Without Fear!* into Polish, Dutch, and Spanish.

In addition to his writing and training, he's a regular contributor for www.FundCoaches.com, a site dedicated to providing affordable, high quality fundraising training for nonprofit leaders and board members.

When he's not helping others get passionate about raising money, he enjoys coffee, homebrewing, reading, and travel. Marc lives in Maine with his incredible wife and three amazing kids. And if you pass him in his car, he'll probably be singing 80's tunes loud enough to embarrass his family.

Find Marc online at:

Twitter: http://twitter.com/marcapitman

Google+: http://bit.ly/MarconGoogleplus

Facebook: http://facebook.com/marcapitman

Ask Without Fear!®

Get the internationally acclaimed book that started it all.

Marc Pitman wrote *Ask Without Fear!* because there were so many causes that could make the world a better place if only they had the funding. So he distilled his years of successful fundraising experience into a fun, practical book ideal for board members and volunteers.

Ask Without Fear! DVD

Marc went into the studio to record the content of *Ask Without Fear!* in a for nonprofit's to use in training their board or staff.

Broken into question-and-answer segments, this series can be viewed in one sitting or referenced when needed.

Get both the book and the DVD on Amazon or at www.FundraisingCoach.com

BOARD RETREAT *Party* PACK

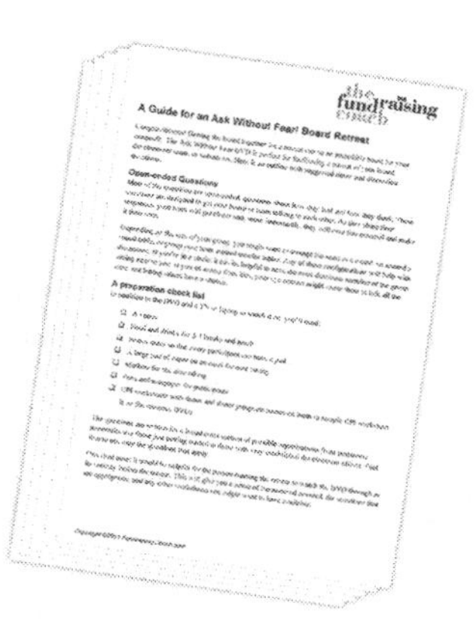

INCLUDES:

1 - "Ask Without Fear" DVD - Includes the get R.E.A.L. training videos
1 - "Ask Without Fear" Resource CD
5 - Board Retreat plan, checklist, and instructional sheets
10 - "Ask Without Fear" Books

More information at

www.BoardRetreatPacks.com

Bulk Orders

To order 10 or more copies for your board or next conference, or to book Marc to speak at your next event, contact him at:

Mail: The Fundraising Coach
8 Waterville Commons Drive, Suite 137
Waterville, ME 04901

Phone: (207) 370-2275

e-mail: marc@fundraisingcoach.com

Website: www.FundraisingCoach.com

16999571R00076

Made in the USA
Charleston, SC
21 January 2013